Grandma's Farm

By Katie Berk
Illustrated by April Hartman

Scott Foresman
is an imprint of

Glenview, Illinois • Boston, Massachusetts • Chandler, Arizona •
Upper Saddle River, New Jersey

Illustrations

April Mosakowski Hartmann.

Photographs

Every effort has been made to secure permission and provide appropriate credit for photographic material. The publisher deeply regrets any omission and pledges to correct errors called to its attention in subsequent editions.

Unless otherwise acknowledged, all photographs are the property of Pearson Education, Inc.

8 Jupiter Images.

ISBN 13: 978-0-328-50777-1
ISBN 10:   0-328-50777-6

7 8 9 10 V010 15 14 13

I love to visit Grandma's farm.
I visit for eight weeks.
I have the best time.

3

I love to do work on Grandma's farm.
I can touch the eggs.

I love the horses on Grandma's farm.
I know how to feed them.
My favorite horse is called Chief.
One day I might get to ride him.

I love to hear about the farm.
Grandma tells funny stories about
when she was a girl.
We laugh a lot.

I love to see the sky on the farm.
We see the moon and stars above.
I love to visit Grandma's farm.

From the Farm to You

Read Together

A lot happens before eggs get to your table. Eggs come from farms. On farms, chickens live in a hen house. It is a large room filled with nests made of hay. Chickens lay eggs in the nests. Farmers collect the eggs and check them. Then they are put in cartons and sent to the grocery store. People go to the grocery store to buy the eggs. Then people cook the eggs, and they are ready to eat.